I Wanted the Elevator, But I Got the Shaft

I Wanted the Elevator, But I Got the Shaft

Inspiration for Life's Ups and Downs

Joe G. Emerson

DIMENSIONS

FOR LIVING

NASHVILLE

I Wanted the Elevator, But I Got the Shaft
Inspiration for Life's Ups and Downs

Copyright © 1993 by Dimensions for Living

All rights reserved.

This book is printed on acid-free, recycled paper.

Illustrated by Charles T. Cox

Library of Congress Cataloging-in-Publication Data

Emerson, Joe G., 1931–
    I wanted the elevator, but I got the shaft : inspiration for life's ups and downs / Joe G. Emerson.
        p.   cm.
    ISBN 0-687-22292-3 (alk. paper)
    1. Christian life—1960– I. Title.
BV4501.2.E44 1993
248.4—dc20   92-45705

Howard Thurman's prayer from *Meditations of the Heart*, Copyright © 1953 (p. 29), is used by permission of Mrs. Howard Thurman.

Most scripture quotations are from the New Revised Standard Version Bible, Copyright 1989 by the Division of Christian Education of the National Council of the Churches of Christ in the USA. Used by permission.
Those noted KJV are from the King James Version of the Bible.

93 94 95 96 97 98 99 00 01 02 — 10 9 8 7 6 5 4 3 2 1

MANUFACTURED IN THE UNITED STATES OF AMERICA

To family and friends,
colleagues and congregations,
defenders and detractors,
with whom I have been privileged
to share experiences and space
on the elevator

Contents

Chapter One

Show Me an Elevator . . .

Elevators are a lot like life: They go up, they go down, and sometimes they are "out of order." Show me an elevator, and I'll show you a symbol that can help us find inspiration for the ups and downs of life.

The Bible is rich in imagery and symbols that help to communicate God's word. The Twenty-third Psalm, for example, uses shepherd imagery to make a strong statement of faith. Jesus also used images and symbols, often through the telling of parables, to help the people of his day grasp new teachings. Most biblical symbols, however, are unfamiliar to us; that is, they come from a time and place that is foreign to us and our experiences. Although we may know what a shepherd is, most of us do not know what it is like to *be* a shepherd. In addition to the symbols of the Bible, we need modern symbols—symbols from our everyday world— that can help us apply those timeless biblical truths to our daily lives.

Show me an elevator, and I'll show you a faith symbol rich in meaning. For most of us in the industrialized countries, elevators are part of the modern world. What better symbol is there to remind us of a faith that sustains us through the ups and downs of life?

Before exploring the ways that elevators and our experiences with elevators can help us to recall the hope and promise of our faith, let me begin by suggesting how the faith journey itself may be compared to an elevator.

Faith Must Be Our Own

I am old enough to remember when elevators were operated by "professionals." No one would have thought of touching the controls. A white-gloved attendant jealously guarded a lever that made the elevator go up and down. We gave the floor number, stood back, and waited for our destination to be announced.

Most of us began our faith journey that way. There was a teacher, or parent, or preacher, or friend, in whose hands we trusted our spiritual well-being. That person taught, and we listened, believed, and were content.

Then there came that day when second-hand religion was not enough. Perhaps it began with a doubt or a question. In any case, there came a moment when we began to realize that we could no longer stand on the promises that were made to someone else. It was not the most comforting moment in our lives.

Jesus experienced this discomfort. He grew up in a tradition of handed-down faith. There came the day when he said, "You have heard that it was said. . . . But I say to you . . ." (Matt. 5:21-22).

When we were children, we enjoyed the luxury of sleeping in the back seat of an automobile on long trips. We knew that a parent or some other adult was in the front seat. We felt safe and confident, knowing that this person was in charge and that all was well. We had no notion of what the future would hold, nor did we much care.

But then we became adults. We no longer were allowed to sleep in the back. We had to drive and be responsible. As Paul wrote, "When I became an adult, I put an end to childish ways" (I Cor. 13:11*b*).

I often speak to people about the *five* Gospels: the Gospels of Matthew, Mark, Luke, John, and Joe. As a matter of fact, if there were no gospel of Joe, there would be no gospel for *me*. That is the gospel I have developed. I have borrowed heavily from the other four, sprinkled it with a bit of the apostle Paul, and added parts from people who have shared their faith with me; and finally, I have claimed it as my own. I have taken the controls of my faith elevator. It is this faith that helps me through the days and nights of my life as I move toward the destinations to which God calls me.

And so it is with all of us. You can't count on anyone else to build your belief system. The Bible certainly shapes it. Your own experience colors it. The traditions by which you were raised impact it. Finally, your mind grapples with it, and it becomes your own. You push the buttons of the elevator of life. It must be so.

Faith Is Not a Plaything

I have seen kids play on elevators, and elevators were not designed for that! Some push all the buttons and get off just to frustrate the others. Some ride up and down just to avoid boredom. That isn't why the elevator is there.

Some people try to play at faith like that. When Paul was preaching in Athens, he poured out from his heart what meant the very most to him. The Athenians remarked that it was an interesting idea that he presented. They invited him to come back another day to discuss it further. They wanted to play at faith. But Paul knew that in every person's life, a faith system is more than an object for casual discussion.

It is important occasionally to run through hypothetical scenarios that begin, "What would you do if. . . ." But it is never quite the same in a real-life situation when real-life people are involved.

I once led a discussion group on the topic of divorce in our society. One older woman confessed, "I used to be so opposed to divorce. I could not condone it under any circumstance. It was not a solution to any marital problem. But I've had to change my mind. My daughter came home battered, bruised, and frightened. She's getting a divorce." This woman knew it was no time for games.

When my father was ninety, he spent the final year of his life with his mind locked in the past. My visits usually consisted of playing the roles of his co-workers on the railroad years ago. Ten years earlier he had needed a pacemaker, and I was now warned that its effectiveness was running out. The doctor suggested that I have the pacemaker regularly monitored to avoid its sudden failure. If necessary, it could be replaced with a new one.

I faced a difficult decision. This was my dad. I loved him. How could I even think about subjecting him to major surgery at his age? On the other hand, I knew that, according to his standards, his present condition was not "living." There was no simple choice. It was no time for games.

It isn't playtime when the harsh realities of life confront us; it is time for serious soul searching and prayer. Faith is not a game to be taken lightly.

One of the most unfortunate characters in the final days of the life of our Lord was Herod. When Pilate sent Jesus to be judged, Herod asked only that Jesus perform a miracle for the amusement of his guests. Herod wanted to play with faith. Jesus refused—and still does.

Faith Is Only a Means, Not an End

One thing is certain: No one is ever going to mistake an elevator for the destination. We get on an elevator to go somewhere. We don't plan to stay on the elevator. But we often have difficulty understanding this about our faith. Faith is only a means by which we grow to feel at home with God.

Third-century theologian Augustine was on target when he said, "God has created us for Himself so that our hearts are restless until we find our rest in Him." Just as an elevator is a means to arrive at a destination, so our faith is the vehicle by which we seek to relieve our restlessness and "come home."

Will Campbell's novella *Cecelia's Sin* tells the story of the Huguenots in a time of persecution. When it seems that all the Huguenots will be killed, Cecelia is asked to record their history. As she is writing the story, the leader of the group, Jacob, reads the opening pages and says, "Cecelia is writing very well, but let us always remember that she is telling the story, and the telling of the story is not the story."

We need to remember that. The Bible is the telling of the story; the Bible isn't the story. The authority of the Bible is the story that is told: God's reaching down to us and our reaching up to God. That's what is important. Faith is the connection, the elevator between us and God, and God is the ultimate bedrock of that faith.

It is easy to mistake the story for reality. It is seductive to put our final faith in the Bible, a system of beliefs, a pet doctrine, or a charismatic leader. Yet these are not the destination; they serve only as elevators to assist us on our way. These vehicles may be very important to our progress, but they fall short of our destination.

I once heard a great preacher say that human beings are born with a blank spot in the center of their beings, in which they must write the name of God. Life is always off-center, unfulfilled, until that blank is finally filled. For some, it is an easy task; for others, it is very difficult; but for all, it is a necessity.

The Good News

We get on an elevator and push a button; the door slides closed, and we trust that we are moving toward our destination. It is a leap of faith. We can't actually see where we are headed.

Our faith journey is like that. We begin it with trepidation about our ultimate destination. We have some assurance, but no certainty. Paul put it honestly when he said that we see in a mirror dimly (I Cor. 13:12).

We are fortunate in getting clues as to our progress along the way, just as numbers light up the floors inside the elevator. This has to be enough. We move by faith. Step by step, floor by floor, we make our way, seeing signs of God's grace along the way.

There is a story about a boy who was afraid of the dark. When his father asked him to go to the barn for a tool, he had to confess his fear. His father handed him a flashlight and told him to shine it toward the barn.

"How far can you see?" the father asked.

"I can see the garage," the boy replied.

"Then go to the garage," the father instructed. "How far can you see now?"

"I can see to the barn-lot gate," the boy answered.

Landmark by landmark, the father led his son to the next goal until at last he reached the barn.

Most of us travel this way on our faith journey—landmark by landmark. What more can we ask? God is faithful and will help us along our journey.

Chapter Two

I Wanted the Elevator, But I Got the Shaft

have been in buildings that were meant to have an elevator but ended up with only a shaft. Perhaps the owner ran out of money and reclassified the elevator as a luxury rather than a necessity. I've even heard of one instance when the architect simply failed to put the elevator on the final instructions to the builder. Once in a while, the elevator is dismissed as superfluous. We all know people whose lives are represented by an empty elevator shaft.

Out of Time

We are people who lead busy lives. We work extra hours. We join numerous organizations. Our children seem to be involved in something every day. A cartoon showing a child waiting for the carpool in hockey uniform when this is swim-class day brings a wry grin from harried parents.

The problem is that we become so involved in so many activities and adventures that time simply runs out. We do not have the power to create thirty-hour days, so we have to figure out what can be eliminated from our twenty-four-hour days. And too often, this is the way we develop our faith.

It seems innocent enough. There will always be time for drawing closer to God, we say, especially when we are in the springtime of our lives and seem to need so little help in living. Sometimes it's fun to climb the stairs even when there is an elevator, just to prove our own strength. Who needs God? Who needs faith? The problem is that we never know when we will need an elevator but will find only a shaft.

Gandhi once was asked when a person should make peace with God. He responded that the ideal time, as far as he could tell, would be one minute before a person dies. When the inquirer protested that no one knows when that moment will be, Gandhi replied, "Then you had better do it now."

We must make sure the elevator is in place before we need it. The time to discover whether a bungee cord is securely attached is before, not after, we leap! The same is true of our faith.

"Too late" is among the saddest phrases in the English language. In a mine disaster near my hometown, twenty miners were trapped deep within one of the tunnels. They were finally reached, but the words "too late" were included in the report. The rescuers were too late to save the miners, but we will never know whether the miners waited too long to find a faith that would sustain them in their final hours.

An urgency about commitment can be found in the Bible. When the prophet Elijah confronted the people of Israel with their waning faith, he cried, "How long will you go limping with two opinions? If the LORD is God, follow him" (I Kings 18:21). Jesus was equally emphatic in his choice of priorities. He taught that entry into the Kingdom was so urgent that we ought to be willing to give up our families to follow him. He even said to a man who wanted to bury his father before leaving home, "Let the dead bury their own dead; but as for you, go and proclaim the kingdom of God" (Luke 9:60). Elijah and Jesus knew how important it is to get started immediately in one's spiritual pilgrimage.

The elevator must be in place before it is needed. Otherwise, only an empty shaft looms ahead.

You Didn't Tell Me!

No contractor is expected to put anything into a building that is not contained in the document from the architect called specifications. There are plenty of horror stories about architectural oversights that have led to embarrassing and sometimes dangerous difficulties. On one university campus there is a beautiful crescent-shaped building. This beautiful building, however, is not air conditioned. No one realized that because all the windows would open outward, all the windows on one whole side of the building would be jammed shut by the shape of the structure. What a mess, and what a shame!

It is also a shame to meet adults who know nothing about faith. The "shaft" that should have been filled with faith stands empty because no one was reponsible for filling it.

In James Michener's *Chesapeake,* a participant in a Quaker wedding says to the young couple, "When thee has children, be sure they are taught to know Jesus. It is a fearful thing to rear children who know not the Christian faith."

As a pastor, I often meet adult inquirers who ask what it means to be a Christian. I begin by asking them what they already know. When they reply "nothing," it breaks my heart. It is indeed a fearful thing to rear children who know not Jesus.

This situation often occurs in families of mixed

faith. Under some misguided notion of letting the children decide for themselves, the parents teach nothing about faith. But the assumption that children must be raised in a spiritual vacuum so that they may make their own faith decisions does not hold true. No matter what we teach them, children ultimately do make their own decisions. But unless we teach them about faith, they have no background from which to draw when making those decisions, and they have no faith support for their early lives.

Jesus said, "It is necessary that temptation come, but woe to those by which it comes." These are stern words of warning to those architects of human lives who neglect to fill the emptiness of the shaft with an elevator of hope!

Extra Baggage?

Sometimes that elevator called faith seems to become extra baggage, at least in our own minds. We think we no longer need faith for our journey. We have hospitals for physical healing and psychologists for mental healing. What is left for us to bring in need to God? What do we need God for? In Aldous Huxley's *Brave New World*, those in charge do not deny the existence of God, but only the relevance of God to life as we know it. In a world in which people and groups who make no claim to act in the name of Christ are caring for the hungry, the needy, the lonely, and the sick, it's no wonder that some may question the relevance of faith in God.

When a certain monarch from the East lost his wife to death, he immediately ordered the finest craftsman to construct a proper casket for her body. When it was completed, he somehow felt it was not enough to express his devotion to her, so he ordered a tomb to house the casket. When even that did not seem to be enough, he built a huge monument to surround the tomb. Still he was not satisfied. Finally he engaged a landscape architect to create a magnificent garden for the finishing effect.

When all was done, the monarch walked through the garden and observed all that he had created. But something bothered him. Something seemed wrong. "It is that ugly thing," he said, pointing to the casket. "Get rid of it. It is out of place in all this beauty."

We slip too easily into seeing the beauty that "good people" do and ignoring the source of that goodness. Unless Jesus Christ is the source of our concern and our good deeds, we eventually grow weary and develop "benevolence fatigue." Jesus was so bold to say that whenever we feed the hungry, clothe the naked, or visit the lonely, we are doing it to him. That gives new meaning to our concern for others. Christ is the source—the elevator, if you will—of our concern for others.

The Good News

There is good news in all this. Even those whose lives appear to be elevator shafts have the necessary "opening"; it is a part of the gift of creation. God created us, crafted us for fellowship with our Creator. The shaft, even if empty, is a part of being human. All we need to do is find an elevator that fits it. That's good news! We are created in God's image, capable, by the fact that we are alive, to find our own way to God. That's a gift.

You cannot say to a tiger, "Thou shalt not kill." It is the nature of a tiger to kill to survive. But it is possible to give the same injunction to a human. We have the ability to choose! It is possible to say to a human,

"Thou shalt love the Lord," because we have a choice. It was built into us.

I want and need an elevator. I know I already have the shaft. I even know some places to begin gathering the parts I will need for the elevator.

And so do you! Why not get started?

Chapter Three

Holding the Door Open

e've all had it happen to us. We are safely aboard the elevator, and we have activated it by pushing the call button for our chosen floor. As the doors begin to close, we see someone coming around the corner who, upon seeing the elevator about to leave, accelerates in order to get aboard. Our instant response is to assist the person. We look quickly and almost desperately for that button on the control panel that says HOLD or OPEN DOOR.

Sometimes we find the button in time and graciously accept the gratitude of our new fellow rider. Sometimes we don't, and we helplessly hear the door click shut and feel the car begin to move. We mutter to ourselves about why all elevators don't have a common marking and a common spot for this important button, and we hope that somehow the stranded would-be rider knows that we really did try.

Life is filled with such instances. Every day we run into someone, friend or stranger, who is hurting or in need. The person may need something as basic as food or as simple as a listening ear. Frequently, his or her plea comes as a complete surprise, calling for a response that is neither reasoned nor calculated. We call someone on the phone and ask, "How are you?" But instead of the requisite answer, "Fine," the person says, "Terrible." We then know that the elevator door is closing, and we had better start looking for the HOLD button!

A Face That Says Yes

The gospel calls us sinners in need of grace, and so we are. We tend to be self-centered, stubborn, and greedy. We tend to take care of ourselves before we worry about anyone else. This is why God sent Jesus to "hold the door"—to place his body between the doors, so to speak, so that we might get aboard. In the process, he was, in the words of Isaiah, "wounded for our transgressions" (Isa. 53:5). Or as Paul wrote, "While we still were sinners Christ died for us" (Rom. 5:8).

Yet despite our sinful nature, we frequently respond positively to others in need. In fact, our instinctive reaction in most instances is to offer help. There is a selfless spark within the human spirit. We see a child fall while skating. We check to see that there is no more damage than a damaged ego. Someone faints at a sporting event. Even during the most exciting part of the game, we offer assistance. A friend calls and asks to have a cup of coffee with us; we hear the S.O.S. in the invitation. We change our schedule to accommodate our friend.

I have difficulty passing by "on the other side" when I see a car parked on the shoulder of the road with its hood up and its emergency lights blinking. I know the potential danger in stopping, so I don't stop. I still feel guilty! It's the only time I regret not having a car phone. I really want to help, and I suspect that most of us feel the same. That's healthy, and that's good news.

This story was told to me about Thomas Jefferson. One day while he was president, he was out riding with a group when they came to a swollen river that a horse could easily cross but a person on foot could not. A man stood beside the water, waiting for someone on horseback to come along and carry him across. He looked up at Jefferson and asked him for a ride. Jefferson agreed. When they got to the other side, someone asked the man why he had picked the president of the United States to carry him across the river. "Because," the man is said to have replied, "there was a look on his face that seemed to say yes."

Jesus must have had that kind of face. When he was speaking to a group of Pharisees at a dinner, a large crowd gathered outside. Suddenly the roof literally opened up, and a man was lowered into the room on a stretcher to be healed. Those who brought the man to Jesus must have seen a look on his face that said, "Yes." And Jesus must have seen a look on the faces of the sick man and his friends that said, "The elevator door is closing, and I need help."

Jesus reacted in the same way whenever he saw the need of others, whether it was a hungry crowd, a group of lepers, or a woman accused of adultery. As Jesus said, whatever we do for the hungry, the naked, the lonely, the sick, or the imprisoned, we are really doing for him. It is in that spirit that we respond.

No Time for Questions

Fortunately, we usually do not have time to decide whether the person rushing toward the elevator is worthy of our assistance. There is no time to ask, "Do you really need to make the trip?" or "Why can't you use the stairs?" or even "Why are you in a hurry?" The person is a human being, and we help.

Again Jesus is our guide. The invalid who was lowered through the roof was not worthy; Jesus' first words to him were, "Your sins are forgiven." But Jesus responded to his need—both his spiritual need and his physical need.

We tend to write rules and develop procedures to keep from being "taken" by those we believe do not deserve our help. What a waste of time and energy! I always assume that the person "on the make" has had more experience cheating others than I have had in preventing it. I can be sure of helping those who need help only by helping a few who don't.

As a child, I fed stale bread to the geese on the local pond. There were a couple of big bad ganders that always got more than their share. They would bear down on the little goslings, scattering them to the wind, and then proceed to gorge. They must have been on another pond when the lesson on sharing was taught. Try as I might, I couldn't feed the rest of the geese without feeding those two old reprobates! The others were hungry. My choice seemed clear; I must feed them all.

We must make sure the needy are cared for, even if that means we have to assist some who may not be deserving.

Finding the Right Button

Just as finding the HOLD button before the elevator doors close is not always easy, so also is doing the right thing as we seek to help others. Part of the struggle is becoming sensitized to the needs of others. When I see a picture of a starving child, I wonder how I would feel if I were the parent. Would I beg? Would I steal? Would I kill? To what lengths would I go to provide food for my child? In this way, I move into the other person's experience.

A surgeon operated on a woman who had a tumor in her cheek. To remove the tumor, he had to sever a nerve. When the young, newly married woman awoke from the anesthetic, her husband was sitting on one side of her bed and the surgeon on the other. Her face was twisted, and the surgeon had to tell her that the damage would be permanent. Hearing the news, she looked up at her husband, wondering what he was thinking.

He said, "It's kinda cute." The surgeon watched as the husband leaned over to kiss his wife, twisting his mouth in the same configuration so that their lips would "match." That husband found the "right button" by moving into the experience and feelings of his wife.

How do you "find the right button" when a friend calls for help and there is no solution to offer? How do you "find the right button" when your friend's wife dies suddenly? The great African American poet-preacher Howard Thurman sent word to such a friend:

> I share with you the agony of your grief,
>> The anguish of your heart finds echo in my own.
> I know I cannot enter all you feel
>> Nor bear with you the burden of your pain;
> I can but offer what my love does give:
>> The strength of caring,
>> The warmth of one who seeks to understand
>> The silent storm-swept barrenness of so great a loss.
> This I do in quiet ways,
>> That on your lonely path
>> You may not walk alone.
>> (*Meditations of the Heart*, p. 211)

When Susie came home from school very late one day, her mother demanded an explanation. She told how her friend's dog had been killed by a car and she had stayed to help. "How did you help?" asked the incredulous mother. "I helped him cry," she replied. She could have done nothing better.

Becoming Involved

There is but one certainty in this drama of life: We need to be willing to get involved. In the story of the good Samaritan, involvement was the thing that set the Samaritan apart from both priest and scribe. He was willing to stop, to see what needed to be done. He had no way of knowing the end result. He only knew that he must stop.

When I was a young preacher, one of my more adventurous church members decided that I needed some thrills in life—and that he had the answer to my need. He would teach me to trail ride on a motorcycle. I had more pride than good sense in those days, so I took him up on the offer. After I had mastered a few elementary procedures like starting, stopping, accelerating, and braking, we plunged into the forest and hit the trail.

My friend kept encouraging me. When I forgot to turn and left the trail, he was patient. When I let the engine die while fording a stream, he suppressed a wicked smile as I waded out of the water. He was still the enthusiast. Then when we finally reached a vista where we could rest, he gave me a great pep talk. He bragged about my steering, my balance, my growing confidence.

Then he looked straight at me and said, "You are making one big mistake. You still try to keep your feet on the pedals. That's all right for road running, but you're never going to ride out here on the trail unless you are willing to get your feet off those pedals and down there in the mud!"

As I've tried to be of assistance to persons along life's way, I have thought of that lesson on the trail. The only people who ever really help are those who are willing to get their feet in the mud—where people really live. We don't need to succeed, we just need to try.

Dr. Oliver Sachs was a young physician whose story is told in the book and movie *Awakenings*. He accepted a position in a mental hospital where patients with encephalitis lethargica were housed. Those affected were completely aware of their surroundings but could not respond in any way.

Appalled that nothing was being done for the patients except custodial care, the doctor began using some experimental drugs. One such drug seemed to work. Patients began to talk. They learned to walk. They danced. They went on field trips. They were reborn. Then the drug began to fail. Slowly, each person returned to the silent prison he or she had known before. Was the experiment a failure? Did the doctor raise false hopes? I say no! Trying to help others—searching for the HOLD button—this is what makes us children of God.

The Good News

It is in moments of crisis that we rediscover the goodness of human beings. We are basically pretty selfish, but there is a spark of the divine that moves among even the worst of us. It shows that we are truly related to God and that goodness can shine through, even when we least expect it. We are related to an infinite God who revealed himself in Jesus Christ, even when we can't admit it.

There is a story about a group of botanists who went to Scotland to study some unusual plant formations there. They were searching the highlands when they looked down in a very narrow crevice and saw an unusual plant blooming. They desperately wanted to take the plant home to study. Their problem was that the crevice was too narrow for any of them to get into. A shepherd was nearby tending sheep, and a small boy was with him.

An idea came to the botanists. They went over and asked the boy, "Son, would you be willing to climb down into that crevice and bring us up a sample of this flower if we tie a rope around your waist?"

After looking down into the crevice, the boy looked at them and said, "Yes, if my father holds the rope."

Yes, when the door begins to close on someone, we can reach out and know that on the other end of the rope is God, and that we are representatives of something far bigger than ourselves. Whether we find the right button or not, we can feel good for having tried.

Chapter Four
Activated by Human Touch

I t was my first grandchild, and in spite of all my assertions that I would not be as foolish as all those other grandpas I had met, I was. I could not resist the gift shop so cleverly located near the elevator to the hospital's maternity ward. I bought. I bought too much—so much that my hands were completely filled, and I had to resort to using the corner of one package to push the call button for the elevator.

Nothing happened. No light came on. There was no indication that the elevator had been summoned. Indeed, the button couldn't even be depressed! It was one of those mechanisms that has no real moving parts. I managed to look through the packages to ascertain the problem, only to discover that this call button was a heat-sensitive device which could be activated only by the touch of a human finger. I had to put down my packages and touch the metal plate with my finger. I suppose my nose would have worked just as well, but not even the giddiness of grandfatherhood could persuade me to be that undignified!

Healed by Touch

I've since thought about that elevator button which requires a human touch, and about how this speaks to our lives in a deeper way. We have a need in this impersonal world to be touched, to know that someone cares enough about us to reach out to us, to be with us. We need that. Specifically, we need the healing power of touch.

You don't need to read many of the Gospel stories of Jesus to discover the healing power of his touch. When Simon Peter's mother-in-law was sick, Jesus touched her hand and the fever left her (Matt. 8:15). He touched the eyes of a blind man, and his sight was restored (Matt. 9:27). Jesus' touch cleansed a leper (Mark 1:41). His touch made the deaf to hear (Mark 7:33).

My favorite story of the power of Jesus' touch is found in Mark 5. Jesus was on an errand of mercy. He was in a hurry. He was on a crowded street. A woman in desperate need managed to get close enough to touch the hem of his garment. Jesus stopped and said, "Someone touched me. I felt the power go out of me." By his touch she was healed.

Jesus invited children to come to him so that he might touch them. On the Mount of Transfiguration, when the three disciples who accompanied Jesus were afraid, he touched them to calm their fears (Matt. 17:7). There is even one incident in which Jesus touched the coffin of a widows only son and restored him to life (Luke 7:14).

Jesus continues to reach out to us today—to touch us with his healing love. We long to be touched, and Jesus meets our need.

Connected by Touch

Touch is a way to express a bond that surpasses words. We are connected to others by touch.

When Michelangelo was attempting to depict the creation of the human race in a painting on the ceiling of the Sistine Chapel, how did he do it? He showed God reaching out a finger to touch the finger of Adam! The

Genesis story makes the touch even more intimate. God breathed into Adam the breath of life. Here was mouth-to-mouth resuscitation, from the very beginning!

God's covenant with Jacob was sealed by a touch. When Jacob wrestled with God by the river Jabok, God touched Jacob, lamed him, and then told him that he would be called Israel. Jacob was blessed by a touch!

When we reach an agreement, we shake on it. It is that handshake, that touch, that is our solemn pledge. Among people of goodwill, it is physical contact that symbolizes a commitment. When someone says, "Let's shake on it," we know we are pledging our word and our honor.

Today, wedding rings are a symbol of marriage, but originally the wedding ring was an indication of property. Only the woman wore the ring. But the marriage ceremony has always included the joining of hands. The pronouncement of marriage still reads to this effect: "Since these two people have consented in holy wedlock and have pledged their faith to each other by the joining of hands and the giving and receiving of rings, I now pronounce them husband and wife"!

In this world in which words have become cheap, there is still a sense in which touch—physical contact—carries a symbolic weight more powerful than reason.

Sustained by Touch

Our need for physical contact to sustain us in time of need has been carefully documented by many disciplines, including medicine. In *The Gift of Touch*, Helen Colton says that the hemoglobin in the blood increases significantly when we are touched. Hemoglobin is that part of the blood which carries vital supplies of oxygen to the heart and brain. She says that if we want to be healthy, we must touch one another.

In hospital nurseries, nurses frequently are instructed

to hold a sick infant for periods of time. Long before words have any meaning, loving care is expressed by touch. The child can sense this gift of caring.

In the church I now serve, we have an abundance of young families, and therefore a bountiful crop of babies. When parents bring a child to be baptized, it is often the case that a fretful and crying infant will become quiet immediately after they have passed the child to me. Some church members think I have a special touch. Others believe that the baby is satisfied by the blessing of baptism. I suspect that neither is true, that the answer is far more commonplace. The baby senses the nervousness of the parents, who want their child to be a perfect angel during the service. That nervousness translates into feelings of danger to the infant. But I am not nervous. I don't mind if the child screams, and somehow that calmness translates into feelings of security. Activated by human touch!

Human touch is the best language of consolation in time of sorrow. I remember the tragic accidental death of the son of a friend who is the president of a Fortune 500 company. The young man and his girlfriend were rushing home to make a curfew and missed a turn in the road. Both died instantly. What could be said? I watched as many friends made feeble attempts at conversation. Then the company's chair of the board arrived. He went immediately to the father and, without saying a word, threw his arms around him.

What a scene. These two men had the authority to make decisions that could affect the lives of thousands of people scattered around the entire world. And they were big men—both were over six feet tall. When they spoke, people listened. Yet in that painful and poignant moment, both knew that words were inadequate, that each felt too deeply to trust his feelings to nouns and verbs. That embrace communicated the feelings of compassion and loss as nothing else could. Activated by human touch!

Touch is the last of our senses to leave us as we drift in illness toward death. Long after patients can no longer hear what is being said to them, and their eyes have ceased to carry messages to the brain, they are aware of being touched. To sit and hold the hand of a loved one during those final hours is a gift of love that never can be measured.

Touch is a gift that sustains us through even the most difficult times.

Good Touch/Bad Touch

Parents and teachers of young children often warn them against sexual dangers by using the good touch/bad touch comparison. Sexual molestation of children is a very real problem in our communities. And sexual harassment is another area of emerging consciousness that has caused many of us to be extremely wary of physical contact. There is no question that unwarranted physical contact with sexual overtones occurs too often in our society, which seems to have become obsessed with sex.

In the more obvious instances, as in pornography, we "know it when we see it"—or feel it. But generally it is not the blatant sexual advances that we have difficulty responding to. It is the honest but misinterpreted touches that cause us to avoid the "appearance of evil." In *Living, Loving, and Learning,* Leo Buscaglia puts it plainly: "One of the saddest things in our culture is that we stress the sexual aspects of a relationship way out of proportion. What a pity, because in those things we are often missing the tenderness, the warmth."

We do not need to give up the warmth of touch. We all know those situations in which touching invites suspicion or personal harm, and we can and should avoid them. But we must freely receive and give the gift of touch, for it is a gift of grace, which enables us to minister to one another.

The Good News

Like many modern elevators, we are activated by human touch, and this is good news, indeed.

I was flying home from a meeting in another city. My practice is to secure an aisle seat and bury my nose quickly in a book. I do not do this because I choose to be unfriendly. It's just such a wonderful opportunity to read and not be interrupted! But on this flight, I could not help being aware of the young woman in the seat next to me. Her level of discomfort at being in an airplane at 30,000 feet was obvious from her blank stare and white knuckles on the armrest.

As we began the descent, she turned suddenly to me and said, "Aren't you afraid?" I assured her that I wasn't and that she needn't be either, and then I turned back to my reading. Her next words were a plea instead of a question: "Do you mind if I hold your hand?" I said I didn't, and she fixed it with an iron grasp.

I could feel her grip become more relaxed. Somehow the touch of another hand gave her confidence. Then the wheels were lowered, and the sound of it raised her anxiety quotient another notch. She turned as best she could in the confines of her seatbelt, threw her arms around me, and buried her head in my chest, smearing lipstick on my shirt and generally giving me an appearance of dishevelment.

I put my arms around her. What else was I going to do with them? We sat that way until the plane was on the ground, taxiing toward the terminal. As we arose to deplane, she said, "Thank you. I could never have made it without you." She then planted a kiss on my cheek that left a trace of lipstick.

She left hurriedly, and I was caught behind other passengers. In my disheveled condition, I left the plane to be greeted by my family. One of them took a look at me and said with just a bit of humor, "It looks like you had an interesting trip." I told them that I had, and I assured them there was an explanation. You may be sure that I was invited to give it!

There is a scene of majestic beauty and power at the conclusion of Dickens' *Tale of Two Cities*. A little girl in a death cart is on her way to the guillotine, and she asks to hold the hand of a condemned man. At the end of the ride to that awful death machine awaiting them, she says to him, "I think you were sent to me by Heaven."

In this elevator we call life, much of human love is activated by touch, by reaching out and feeling the warmth, concern, and support of someone else. Don't be too proud to receive it. Don't be too afraid to share it.

Chapter Five

Going in the Wrong Direction

t has happened to all of us. We get on an elevator and push the button for our destination. The doors close, and the elevator begins to move. Although we can't see anything outside this little cubicle, the movement of our internal organs tells us that we are going in the wrong direction.

Most often it happens by accident. We didn't pay attention to the direction arrow before we boarded. Once in a while, though, we purposely get into a crowded elevator, no matter what direction it is moving, simply to get a space. But one thing is certain: We are not going to get to where we want to be!

Life is often like that. We are headed in the wrong direction, whether intentionally or unintentionally, and it is certain that we are not going to get to where we want to be.

In Pursuit of Happiness

You can walk up to almost any person you know and ask what he or she wants most in life, and the answer will be some variation of "I want to be happy." Our forebears even wrote this dream into the Preamble of the Constitution, as an inalienable right to life, liberty, and the pursuit of happiness.

We take the promise of life and liberty fairly casually. Most of us expect to live our fourscore and ten in a free country. This expectation is incredible when compared to other parts of the world. I was participating in a retreat held at a center that was in the flight pattern of practicing jet fighter planes. The scream of their approach and the roar of their afterburners made conversation impossible. After a particularly frustrating moment, one of our group brought us back to reality by pointing out that it is great to live in a country where the early-morning sounds of arriving jets raise only frustration levels, not fear.

We rejoice in our liberty, although we know we have abused its freedom. Still, we continually use our freedom to take off in the wrong direction, and then we wonder why we are not happy. Often it is the pursuit of happiness that gives us the most trouble in life.

Wealth

In our culture, we tend to believe that the acquisition of things brings happiness. We think that if only we were a little more wealthy—if only we had a better house, or car, or boat—then we would be happy.

Has it ever occurred to you that we live in a "button culture"? All the many appliances and gadgets we buy have buttons. We are judged by the number of buttons we can afford.

The washing machine at my house has seven buttons, but I don't think we have ever used more than four of them. Our dishwasher has eight buttons. We preset three and forget the other five. To the best of my knowledge, our dishes have never figured out that they are missing some subtle shift in water temperature or scrubbing action by this omission on our part!

Make your own button count. How many unused buttons do you have on your stove, your blender, your microwave, your TV, your stereo, your computer, your calculator, your car?

I have a friend who bought a particular car because it has a special feature. The lights go off automatically soon after the ignition is turned off. Although most of us might like such a feature, my friend has decided that it is unnecessary—and a bit of a nuisance. He gets yelled at all the time by well-meaning people who think he has forgotten to turn off his lights. And he cannot remember ever having run down a battery because he had left his lights on!

Jesus told a story of a rich man who had several barns and thought he would be happy if only he could have bigger ones. Then and only then, he thought, could he take his ease. But God said to him, "You fool! This very night your life is being demanded of you. And the things you have prepared, whose will they be?" (Luke 12:20). If Jesus were telling this story today, perhaps he might talk of the buttons and gadgets we seem to need to prove that we have arrived.

Jesus was not against wealth. He even had some rich friends. One let him use his villa for Holy Week. One loaned him a donkey. One even gave him his tomb! But Jesus was aware of the seductive power of wealth. Jesus' stories such as the parables of the rich fool (Luke 12:13-21) and the rich ruler (Luke 18:18-30) were not told to present positive role models, but to illustrate the seductive power of wealth.

Escape

In addition to our compulsive fascination with material wealth, our culture seems to have a compulsive fascination with escapism. Thinking that escaping from our troubles will bring happiness, many of us turn to drugs or alcohol. How many times have we heard that getting high on these crutches causes the world to look a little better and people to be a little more pleasant? "It's a jungle out there, and I need something to take the edge off," we reason.

Of course, turning to addictive substances or behaviors is a foolish diversion in the wrong direction. At best, we wake up the next morning with nothing different— except that we have a headache! At worst, we destroy our lives.

Stephen Foster wrote so many songs that are vibrant, alive, and joyful: "Oh, Suzanna," "Camptown Races," "Old Folks at Home," "My Old Kentucky Home." But his personal life was quite a contrast. Foster was an alcoholic. He didn't finish school. He couldn't hold a job. His one great love was Jeannie, the one "with the light brown hair." They were divorced after a brief marriage. In 1864, at age thirty-eight, he died in the Bowery with only a few cents in his pocket. Someone once remarked that Foster had the melody but could never find the words. I say he got on the elevator of life and headed in the wrong direction.

Success

Success is another of those high-risk goals that can head us in the wrong direction. How important we think it is to "get ahead." All of us have known those who were willing to do anything and step on anyone to achieve the goal for which they strived. But hurting others, and ultimately ourselves, is not worth the kind of society we create in the process.

The Girl Scouts recently commissioned the Harris Group to poll opinions of teenagers. Sixty-five percent of the teenagers polled said they would cheat on a test if it meant passing it. That's going in the wrong direction!

Two officers in a major city's police force were so desperate to be promoted that they had failing test scores overturned by arguing that because everyone cheated on the tests, it would be unfair to deprive them of their equal rights. That's going in the wrong direction!

Although he has turned his life around and now is a bold witness for Jesus Christ, few will forget the quote attributed to Charles Colson when he was the political advisor for Richard Nixon: "I would step on my mother in order to see the president reelected."

Another aspiring politician said to me one day, "No matter how noble your goals, you can do nothing if you don't get elected. I plan to do anything, and I do mean anything, to be elected."

The examples are endless. The tragedy is that we generally know where we are going. We live with the prodigal in us who says to his father, "Give me my share of the inheritance" and proceeds to head to the far country in search of happiness. Like the prodigal, who knowingly gave up the love and security at home, we too make our choices and head in the wrong direction.

Stephen King's mystery novel *Needful Things* is based on an interesting twist. Someone sets up a shop where it is possible to purchase *anything*. The only problem is that you cannot use money. The only barter exchange in this little shop is your soul. The book is symbolic of our willingness to give whatever it takes to have what we think will bring us happiness. We head in the wrong direction to look for happiness or meaning.

Why is it that once we get over the original shock of the elevator going in the wrong direction, we so easily make our peace with it? We become entrapped while still believing we are in control. A very good chess player once gave me a sad lesson. I thought I was distinguishing myself pretty well against his superior knowledge of the game. Then quietly he told me that I was defeated. I started to protest, but he showed me the inevitable flow of the game. He then told me that I had made my strategic error ten moves earlier. I wasn't even aware of it. That's a major problem for many of us. We go too far in the wrong direction before we become aware of where we are.

Like Br'er Rabbit in the Uncle Remus stories, we continue to hit the tar baby until we can no longer extricate ourselves.

Where Are You Going?

If you wonder occasionally about your own sense of direction, I refer you to two important books: your datebook and your checkbook. Take a look at how you spend your time and money.

The more difficult to track is the datebook. To our dismay, we are confronted with the truth that time is irreplaceable. I skipped an important gathering in order to be present when my year-old grandson went to see a special Christmas display. Then my daughter, rather undiplomatically, reminded me that she couldn't remember that I had done the same for her. My lame reply was that perhaps I had learned something in the interim. But the fact remains that I had allowed my datebook to keep me from sharing a significant experience in my daughter's life.

On Sunday evenings, my wife, Gloria, and I invite people to our home as a way to get acquainted with individuals in our church. One of the questions we ask is, "What do you like to do in your spare time?" Too many say they have no spare time! This is true for many of us: Our datebooks are full. Unfortunately, when we "take inventory" of our datebooks, we often do not like the priorities reflected there.

Just as our datebooks tell us something about the direction we are headed, so our checkbooks reveal our "sense of direction." An Internal Revenue Service agent audited a wealthy businessman who also happened to live in the same neighborhood. After the completion of the audit, the agent invited the man to go to church with him some time. The man replied that he was already an active member of a church. The agent tried to conceal his look of surprise. He had assumed that the man was not an active church member because of his poor record of giving.

A former parishioner told me the story of his promotion in business. He married the daughter of a wealthy industrialist and worked many years in the business. One day his father-in-law called him in and said that he was going to make him president of the company, and he asked, "Do you want to know why I have decided to do this?"

The answer seemed obvious to my friend. He replied, "I have worked hard. I have been loyal. I married your daughter, and you have no sons."

The father-in-law replied, "While all of that is true, it would not be enough. I've watched you through the years. You have learned what it means to give. To me, that is the most important lesson of life."

My friend's life is a testimony to this truth. Whenever there is a worthy cause to be supported, you can be sure that both his checkbook *and his datebook* reflect his commitment.

It's never easy to judge ourselves as we seek a direction for our lives. We too easily raise convincing arguments to justify almost any action. But sometimes we have to come to terms with the "wrongness" of our direction and head back home.

In *Lake Wobegon Days*, Garrison Keillor tells the story of a man who was sitting at home one evening when a snowstorm came out of the northwest. He realized he was out of cigarettes and, upon having a nicotine fit, decided he would drive to town in spite of the storm. He was in trouble almost as soon as he left home. He managed to get to the store and buy the cigarettes, but by then the wind was howling and the snow was falling so hard that he was afraid he would not be able to get back home. He wasn't. He ended up in a snowbank by the side of the road with the car turned over on its side. Keillor wrote:

> A pretty dumb trip. Town was a long way to go in a blizzard for the pleasure of coming back home. He could have driven his car straight to the ditch and saved everyone the worry. But what a lucky man. Some luck lies in not getting what you thought you wanted but getting what you have, which once you have it you may be smart enough to see is what you would have wanted had you known. He takes deep breaths and the cold air goes to his brain and makes him more sensible. He starts out on the short walk to the house where people love him and will be happy to see his face.

Take a look at *your* datebook and checkbook. What do they tell you about your priorities? Are you headed in the right direction?

The Good News

This is the good news: We don't need to continue in the wrong direction. The first step is admitting that we are headed in the wrong direction. We are truly sorry for what we have done, and we confess our sin. The scripture says that if we confess our sin, God is quick to forgive us. Then we are ready to actually turn ourselves around. The biblical word for this step is *repentance*. The literal translation of the word *repent* means "to turn around" or "to change direction." When we repent, we change our direction by doing something to correct the situation.

When the prodigal "came to himself" and realized he had managed to mess up royally, he did something to change his direction. He prepared a speech for his father to acknowledge his unworthiness, and he headed home. But before he could even give his speech, his father welcomed him with open arms. He was more than willing to have his son back home where he belonged.

A word of caution for those seeking painless solutions: Although the prodigal was received back into his father's house, his inheritance was gone. He had squandered it. There is a price for going in the wrong direction. But the good news is that we can change our direction; we can be forgiven.

Changing our direction forces us back to the Book we call holy. In the book of the prophet Micah are these words of wisdom: "What does the LORD require of you but to do justice, and to love kindness, and to walk humbly with your God?" (Mic. 6:8). That's plain enough.

Jesus said, "Strive first for the kingdom of God and his righteousness, and all these things will be given to you as well" (Matt. 6:33). Jesus is terribly concerned that we head in the right direction—in short, that our priorities are straight. And he is there to help us find our way. That is good news, indeed.

Chapter Six

Getting Off on the Wrong Floor

 suspect that anyone who uses elevators has, at one time or another, gotten off on the wrong floor. You push the call button for your floor. The elevator stops. Paying no attention, you jump out, and when you look around, you realize that you are on the wrong floor.

I remember the first time it happened to me. I could not have been more than seven or eight years old. I was headed for the sports floor in a department store, talking excitedly to a friend about a baseball mitt I wanted to show him. The elevator stopped. Out we went into women's lingerie! In those days, the lingerie department was off limits to young boys. Two very red-faced boys climbed back on the elevator, to the amusement of our fellow passengers.

It certainly wasn't the last time I made that error. I have done so in office buildings, in hospitals, and in hotels. I know by now that it is not a major disaster. The most dire result is embarrassment.

Life is sometimes like that. We join an organization, only to find out we don't belong there. We speak a word that unintentionally hurts someone—the look on his or her face tells us. Generally, these are easily correctable mistakes on our part. All we have to do is say, "I'm sorry."

Acknowledging the Little Mistakes

Getting off on the wrong floor may be embarrassing, but it's a little mistake, something we can get over quickly—unless we can't admit that we've gotten off on the wrong floor. Something inside us says, "I am the kind of person who makes no mistakes." Or perhaps we overlook the little mistakes. It's always the little misunderstandings that get us into trouble—an off-hand comment that hurts somebody's feelings, or perhaps our lack of courtesy. But unless we acknowledge these little mistakes and take action to rectify them, they become big mistakes.

Years ago, when my wife and I were new faces at the university where I attended seminary, a senior from our home state of Indiana greeted me. We chatted about the towns in our state that we both were familiar with. It was good to talk to someone from "home." He said, "My wife and I would like you and Gloria to come over to our house for dinner sometime." We talked about it and then set a date. He said, "I will check with my wife to see if this date is OK, and I'll let you know the time." I said OK and wrote myself a reminder.

As the day came closer, he didn't say anything to me about the time nor whether he had talked about it with his wife. Gloria and I wondered whether we should call them. But in our culture, you don't call someone and say, "When was it you wanted us for dinner?" So we waited and waited, and finally the day came when we were supposed to go. We decided we'd stay home. If they discovered they hadn't told us a time, they'd call us and say, "Where are you?" and we'd say, "We're on our way."

They didn't call. The next time I saw him, I thought

he was a little less friendly than he had been before. To this day, I still don't know whether I misunderstood him or he misunderstood me. At any rate, that minor incident kept us from having two new friends. It was a silly, correctable mistake.

In the Bible, there is a love poem called the Song of Solomon. In that love poem is a phrase concerning the destruction of love: "Catch us the foxes, the little foxes, that ruin the vineyards" (Song of Sol. 2:15). Major problems can be acknowledged, worked on, and usually solved. It's the little problems that we ignore.

I knew a couple whose marriage got off to a bad start because of a foolish oversight. The wife came from a family that enjoyed celebrating birthdays. This extended far beyond the immediate family to aunts, uncles, cousins, and, I suspect, some interlopers. Ice cream, cake, and presents were plentiful. The celebrations may have been excuses for the group to gather, but that family sure knew how to mark birthdays. The closest relative was always the organizer of the festivities.

The new husband knew nothing of this tradition. His family's tradition was to acknowledge the passing of another year with a card—if they remembered to send it. Their family celebrations did not center around birthdays.

Unfortunately, the wife's birthday came first after their wedding. When no plans were announced, she was sure that her husband planned a surprise. His plan, however, was to take her to a quiet dinner, just the two of them. She was confident that when they arrived at the restaurant, her family would jump out and cry, "Surprise! Surprise!" They didn't. By the time the day was over, there was a chill in the house—and it was not caused by the weather!

The poor husband didn't find out what was wrong

55

for a long time. What began as a simple and correctable mistake was magnified into a major marriage crisis.

It is indeed the little foxes that spoil the vineyard. Small mistakes or misunderstandings hinder our faith journey. We think we have it all figured out. Then something happens that doesn't fit. We're not quite sure whom we should talk to—or even if we should talk to anyone at all. We don't know if we should pray more or stop altogether.

In *The Screwtape Letters,* C. S. Lewis's tongue-in-cheek story about Satan coaching little devils who try to lead humans down the primrose path to hell, the best advice Satan gives to these charming little tempters is that "the safest road to hell is always a gradual one, a gentle slope, soft underfoot, without any sudden turnings, without milestones, without signposts." When we ignore or deny the little mistakes, we begin to gradually drift from the right path.

There is a story about a wealthy woman who lived in a mill town. It was her town; she owned the mill. The people worked for her. It was a warm kind of benevolent dictatorship.

As she approached her sixty-fifth birthday, she decided she wanted to give something back to the town. She would throw a party and invite everybody in town into her home. She wanted them to know she loved them. So she addressed an individual invitation to every person in the town.

The big day came. She had all the food prepared. No one came. She was hurt. Then she was angry. Then she became furious. Then she decided that the town didn't deserve her, and she'd never show her face there again. She didn't. She stayed home and turned inward on herself.

When she died, two weeks passed before anyone knew, because she was all alone in her home. As people began to clean out the house, they discovered all those invitations in a drawer in her desk. She'd forgotten to mail them! No one would ever know whether she had discovered her mistake but couldn't bear to acknowledge it. Just think, one word to one person—asking *Why?*—could have prevented this tragedy.

Getting off on the wrong floor doesn't get us into major difficulties. It is our unwillingness to admit our mistake that causes the trouble. Small incidents find lodging in our minds and become magnified way out of proportion.

Seeking Reconciliation

The book of Acts tells of an argument between Paul and Barnabas about whether John Mark should be allowed to accompany them on their second missionary journey. This quarrel escalated to the separation of the two because neither could give in. Think what was lost. Barnabas had been Paul's mentor. They had risked their lives in their first missionary journey. Now they went their separate ways because of what seems to be a minor disagreement. There is no evidence in the Bible that they ever reconciled. What a tragedy, which could have been averted quickly and simply! Add to this the irony that John Mark, whom Paul dismissed so emphatically, ended up in Rome as one of Paul's associates. What needless grief for these two giants of our faith.

Jesus spoke urgently about quick reconciliation. He taught that if a person went to the temple to present an offering and had something against his or her brother or sister, the person was first to go and make amends (Matt. 5:24). Since people were expected to worship each week, Jesus was reminding them to reconcile quickly. He was telling them, and us, not to let the matter go unattended. The further from the event or hurt we get, the harder it is to make amends.

One day I was talking to a man whose hatred for his neighbor was well known in the community. I asked him what started the quarrel. He started to tell me and then began sputtering. Suddenly he confessed that he couldn't remember! Somewhere back in a forgotten time, one of them had hurt the other. This had escalated into a war of words and then years of silence. That's judgment. We want so badly to justify our actions! It always fails.

Getting off on the wrong floor is no big deal on an elevator or in life. It is a common occurrence. Staying there is the disaster.

Simon Peter was confident that he would never deny Jesus. But Jesus knew better. When Peter found himself in the high priest's courtyard, during the kangaroo court taking place inside, three times he denied that he knew Jesus. And the cock crowed. "The Lord turned and looked at Peter. . . . And [Peter] went out and wept bitterly" (Luke 22:61-62). Peter's healing began in the midst of those bitter tears, when he admitted to himself that he had failed. Later, after the resurrection, he would have the opportunity to reconcile himself to Christ.

There is something about acknowledging an honest mistake and saying "I'm sorry" that heals us. In the 1992 World Series between Montreal and Atlanta, the United States Marine color guard unintentionally carried the Canadian flag into the Atlanta stadium upside down. An international situation threatened as Canadians were angry at what appeared to be an insult. The President of the United States apologized. Canadians were urged not to retaliate. The best moment came, however, when the announcer at the first game in Montreal said over the PA system that the United States Marine color guard had asked permission to be the flag bearer so that they could carry the Canadian flag correctly. You could actually see people begin to relax, and even smile a bit.

The ability to admit a mistake goes a long way toward keeping cherished relationships. Even if you believe strongly that what you did was correct, a lot of unnecessary grief can be avoided when you can say with integrity, "I'm sorry I hurt you."

The Good News

The Bible is so very honest about our frailties. I wonder how things might have been different if Adam and Eve had expressed regret instead of excuses when they were caught with apple juice on their chins.

I wonder what slight, real or imagined, caused Cain's anger to begin and grow to such a level that he would murder his own brother, Abel.

I wonder what childish miscue came between David and his son, Absalom, and led to insurrection and death.

There must have been an early moment when reconciliation would not have been a monumental undertaking.

Take your cue from Peter. He got off on the wrong floor, only in his case it was the courtyard of the high priest's house. He denied that he knew Jesus—not once but three times. The cock crowed. Jesus turned and looked at Peter. Peter had the grace to cry and the good sense to return to his Master.

We all get off on the wrong floor of life occasionally. And when we do, we must admit it, correct it, and move on!

Chapter Seven

Elevator Etiquette

There were so many people crammed into the elevator that some graciously volunteered to wait for the next one. No one had pushed the call button to get off on the second floor. We stopped anyway. There stood a rather massive man who, even when no one departed, said cheerfully, "Looks like you've got room for one more!" and proceeded to shove his way aboard, depleting what little space remained between bodies and leaving us feeling like kosher dills in a jar. *What nerve!* I thought.

At the very next floor, a thin voice piped up: "This is my floor. Out please." We all poured out of the elevator to allow her to leave. As she proceeded, I recognized her as the one who almost knocked people out of the way for fear she wouldn't get into the elevator at the first floor. Now, since she was well into the elevator, she had to disrupt everyone to get out. If this bothered her, it did not show.

Elevators can bring out the best in people—or the worst. There are few concrete rules for elevator behavior, and absolutely no enforcement officers. Although our elevator behavior generally falls into patterns and practices, we are always subject to one individual who insists on his or her own way. All of us have seen someone take possession of the control panel as if he or she had some hidden need to be in charge, at least for that short ride. We have seen others who will never trust anyone to push the button for their floor and must do it themselves. And then there is the one who must be last in and first out, like a railroad conductor.

Our world and the people in it remind me of this elevator phenomenon. There are few rules that seem to be universally accepted. Our customs are often in conflict. We have traditions, but they seem transitory. We talk of values and soon learn that the method by which we determine them leads us to difficult conclusions about their merits.

Still we share this elevator called earth. We pass one another as we go to and from our daily tasks and, for a while at least, share common space. We are dependent on some generally accepted behaviors in these limited confines, and we must give some care to the vehicle itself.

Caring for the Equipment

As Christians, we believe that God created the earth, populated it with all that was necessary for life, and gave the human race dominion over all the rest. At least that is what it says in the creation story in Genesis. Just how this is to be worked out in the best interests of the creatures that have been given dominion and those that are under our care is a continuing struggle. A childhood experience with picking strawberries helped me sort it out.

My father was a gardener. He loved to get out in his acre of ground and grow things. His gardens not only needed to produce but they also had to look perfect. Rows were plowed along lines to assure straightness. Weeds were treated as felons worthy of capital punishment. *Better Homes and Gardens* could have used his garden as a cover photo.

In that garden he had a strawberry patch. I'm sure he never looked in the encyclopedia to discover that a strawberry is classified as a weed! Perhaps even then, he would have given it a reprieve because of the delicious fruit it surrendered in the spring of the year.

Dad assumed (erroneously in those early years of my life) that I shared his enthusiasm for gardening. At least he thought that whenever he was working in the garden, I should be there as well. I was!

When strawberry picking time came, we worked together. He laid down the rules, and the rules seemed to favor the patch. As we slowly worked our way down the rows, we were first to pull all weeds. We were to avoid stepping on any plant. Dead leaves and diseased berries were to be picked with as much care as the perfect fruit. It seemed to my young mind that receiving the harvest was absolutely secondary. We *always* left a picture-perfect patch. We *sometimes* ate strawberries.

But now, "fast forward" to my teenage years, when the pick-your-own farms became common. With labor costs rising, many farmers raised all kinds of fruits and vegetables and opened their fields for amateurs to harvest the produce at reduced prices. Early converts to this sort of marketing were the strawberry patches, because they defied any mechanical means of harvesting.

I was among the first visitors to such patches. The reason was simple: I liked strawberries, and a little sweat equity was greatly rewarded. The behavior of the pickers, however, is what has remained with me. The "picker's code" is best described as pick the best and leave the rest! There was no regard for the plants at all. They were trampled, pulled, torn, and generally abused by all. We didn't worry about whether there would be anything left for the next pickers, and certainly didn't feel any responsibility to the owner. We filled our boxes with the best we could find, paid, and left.

Press "fast forward" again. I was serving my first church when a good friend made me an offer. He was retired and was planning a major trip during the spring. He had a beautiful strawberry patch, and he said that if I would take care of it, I could have all the strawberries it produced. I felt honored and blessed at the same time. Like my father, he was proud of his garden. He trusted me to care for it as he would. In turn, I received all the bounty of his careful preparation, and I worked hard to see that his trust was not misplaced. No "picker's code" this time. That spring was a good one for both of us.

When we look at this elevator called earth, we recognize that we have the use of it for only a short time. We have inherited it from others who saw to it that it was here for our use. We need to leave it in good condition.

At the same time, it is here for our use. "Have dominion" is the inspiration of God to Adam. We are stewards of this magnificent creation, and we are to be grateful.

Rules for the Ride

How do we get along with one another inside this elevator called earth? The space seems limited. There are lots of us. We come in all shapes and sizes, colors and creeds, beliefs and belongings. We don't always agree; in fact, we have been known at times to be pretty violent in our disagreements.

We vaguely understand that since there is only one elevator, we dare not destroy it. This deterrent has, on occasion, stifled the enthusiasm with which we have pursued our aggressiveness. But this understanding has not contained our aggressiveness completely, and we cannot seem to find a way of getting a handle on it. There isn't an easy button to push to make human relationships easy, and when we begin to survey the problem, we want to throw our hands up in surrender.

Although there is not an easy solution, I believe we

can, without too much controversy, find a common beginning. I am of the pre-computer generation. Believing that I ought to somehow "get with it," I purchased one. The purchase included lessons. An unexpected move placed me with the computer in one city and the lessons in another. So I decided to teach myself. I opened the manual and thumbed through it, but I couldn't even understand the vocabulary. I was absolutely lost!

Then I turned to the first page and read, "First you turn the computer on." That I could do! I could also read the next step, and then the next. I still do not have all the answers, but I know a few things that make the computer useful to me.

Surely we can figure out some simple rules for living with others in this elevator called life. We can begin with the understanding that God loves all the children of the world and declares all of us to have infinite worth. Jesus spoke of God's concern for even the birds of the air: "Are you not of more value than they?" (Matt. 6:26). This tiny affirmation moves us a colossal step toward the way we should treat one another. It seems logical and fairly simple to infer that if God declares every person to be valuable, then we as followers can do no less. We should, therefore, treat everyone we come in contact with as a valuable person. When we recognize the worth of others, we have a new outlook on life.

I can no longer read statistics without seeing faces. I remember a census taker who called on a mother of a large family and asked how many children she had. She replied, "Let's see, there's John, Sally, Sam, Judy—" When he interrupted with some impatience, "I don't need names. I only want numbers," she responded, "But they are not numbers; they are people."

The Golden Rule tells us how to live out this understanding. Every culture and religion has within it some version of the Golden Rule. The statements may vary, but they all say that our life's journey would be far more pleasant if we would treat others in the same way we wish to be treated—as persons of worth.

Living by the Golden Rule means that when someone needs to get on the elevator, those of us on board are to find room. In some cases, this involves some inconvenience and, perhaps, even sacrifice. It can also mean that on occasion we will need to concede that someone else is in more urgent need than we are, and we should acknowledge that we can wait for the next trip.

Living by the Golden Rule also means that our desires, which we usually call our rights, must give way at some point to the common good. We are not allowed to smoke on an elevator. It is logical to accept the fact that someone's selfish desire to pollute the air on earth for his or her own economic gain should be limited. So we must recognize also that our selfish desires in the elevator of life often are harmful to others and, therefore, should become secondary to the well-being of others.

Which others? we often are tempted to ask. Does this mean *everyone?* When Jesus was asked which was the greatest Commandment, he replied that we should love God first of all and love our neighbor as ourself (Luke 10:26). When pressed about who this neighbor should be, he told a story about a despised Samaritan (Luke 10:29-37). In elevator language, Jesus meant *every* occupant, regardless of race, nationality, or social standing.

The Good News

I have neither the time nor the knowledge to solve the many complex social problems of our world. There are more questions than I could even begin to answer. What changes will affect the family? What will become of the debate about the beginning and end of human life? How shall we be evangelists for the Christian faith in the midst of other strongly held, ethically based faiths? I must leave these and other questions to persons more expert than I. With the apostle Paul, I confess that I see in a mirror dimly, and I know that my knowledge is imperfect (I Cor. 13:12). But I do know that love is the beginning, and this is good news.

Paul writes in First Corinthians: "Love is patient; love is kind; love is not envious or boastful or arrogant or rude. It does not insist on its own way; it is not irritable or resentful; it does not rejoice in wrongdoing, but rejoices in the truth. It bears all things, believes all things, hopes all things, endures all things" (13:4-7). A person who subscribes to this belief is one I'd like to share the ride with. Therefore, I need to be that kind of person.

Love is a start. It is a beginning on which we can build. We will make mistakes. But we can always come back to step one—and that step is love.

When I came to the end of this chapter, I thought about renaming it. *Etiquette* seems a feeble word to describe some of the issues we have edged up to. So I looked the word up in the dictionary. It says that etiquette is the form required by good breeding to be observed in social life. There are many definitions of "good breeding," but I like to think of it as the new birth which Jesus spoke of to Nicodemus:

No one can see the kingdom of God without being born from above. . . . And this is the judgment, that the light has come into the world, and people loved darkness rather than light because their deeds were evil. For all who do evil hate the light and do not come to the light, so that their deeds may not be exposed. But those who do what is true come to the light, so that it may be clearly seen that their deeds have been done in God.

(John 3:3, 19-21)

Jesus is telling us how to behave on the elevator of life. We are to behave as new creations—born from above—whose actions are grounded in love. How rewarding the "ride" is when we follow the example of Christ!

Chapter Eight

Out of Order

The elevator is one of the many mechanical items in my life that I take for granted. When I get in my car and turn the key, I expect it to start. If it doesn't, I somehow feel betrayed. When I turn on the TV, I want it to be ready to deliver the picture. When it doesn't, I am embarrassingly irritated. When I go into a building and need an elevator, I expect it to be waiting and ready.

When I rush into a building, running a little late, step briskly up to the elevator bank, and see that little sign that says "out of order," I want to scream, "What do you mean 'out of order'? I need you, and I need you now!"

That happens to a lot of us in our life experiences. We run into a situation that requires a faith response, but our faith is "out of order."

A young man who is faithful in his prayers, confident in God's love, and blessed by athletic gifts that should take him all the way to professional sports is in an automobile accident. His athletic career is over. What of his faith? Did he not believe in God? Why did this happen?

A family went to church every Sunday and said a prayer at every meal. They were the picture of the solid family. They knew what being religious was all about. Then their son was caught in a drug bust. What happened? Had they not done what was required of them?

Had they not been taught that God would take care of them?

What do we do when the elevator of faith we have counted on breaks down?

Sometimes We Curse the Elevator

Some people curse the elevator for not being in working order when they need it. Some even go so far as to kick it! Most people get very angry at the broken contraption, or angry at the one who has an office so high that it can't be reached without using the elevator.

Sometimes we also become angry when our cherished beliefs break down, when those beliefs or people in whom we have believed are different from reality.

Judas Iscariot is a classic example. Judas joined the disciples' band with the idea that Jesus was the Messiah who was going to free Israel from the heels of the boots of Rome, the Messiah who was going to be a political hero.

Then on Palm Sunday, Judas discovered that he and Jesus were not reading the same parts of the scripture. Jesus was reading passages from the prophet Isaiah, passages about a suffering servant, about the Messiah who would come, one who would be wounded for our transgressions and by whose bloody back we would be healed—who would come to us, not as one who conquers but as one who suffers, and in that suffering, leads us to God. Judas couldn't take it. He cursed the moment he ever got involved. He became so angry at Jesus, this vehicle to reach God, that he lashed out and betrayed him.

Sometimes our cherished beliefs do not help us in time of trouble. There is a scene in Olive Ann Burns' *Cold Sassy Tree* in which Grandpa is praying for Granny, who is desperately ill. Will Tweedy, the grandson, along with the rest of the community, also is praying that Granny will get well. But she doesn't get well. She dies, and Will is angry, angry about the time he spent praying, angry at God for not answering his prayer the way he wanted. Later he says to his grandfather, "Prayer's no good. Jesus said, 'Ask God for something and you'll get it.' "

And Grandpa said to him, "Thet was jest wishin'. It warn't prayin'." There's a difference.

Belief is something we develop with our minds. It's creedal; it's something we recite on Sunday mornings. It's something that gets hammered or chiseled into us as we grow. It is a fair-weather discipline. *Faith* is altogether different. Faith is what we need when the storms come. We stake our life on a belief, but it is faith that trusts the belief. So we curse the beliefs. We get mad at the elevator and we get mad at God.

Anger simply does not help. James Weldon Johnson began his sermon poem "The Prodigal Son" with this line: "Young man, young man, your arm's too short to box with God."

Anger at a flawed belief system may be understandable, but not very helpful. The "out of order" sign is still there, and we are still in need.

Sometimes We Say It Doesn't Matter

Sometimes when confronted with a broken-down elevator, or with a broken-down belief system, we con ourselves into thinking we didn't need the elevator anyway. Our need to get from here to there is lost in our frustration over the vehicle. We say it doesn't matter. We want to just forget it and leave.

Didn't Jesus promise that we would be granted anything we ask in his name? Didn't he say that if we had enough faith, we could move mountains? If that isn't true, what's the point in believing anything?

A child announced to her parents that she was never going to pray again. When asked why, she responded,

"It does no good. My hair is still straight, Uncle Charlie did lose his job, and the cat died!" I have little doubt that this child's prayers were offered in complete confidence. It was not lack of faith that caused a breakdown. It was a faulty foundation of belief.

Chicago was built on the sandy shores of Lake Michigan. Nearly a hundred years ago, a skyscraper called the Columbus Building was erected. It soared above the city but began to sink into the ground. When it was shored up on one side, it would sink on the other. Finally it had to be torn down. It was impossible to find any way to save it from the shifting sands.

Geologists did further research. By the time the Prudential Building was erected, they knew what it took to build a skyscraper in Chicago. Pilings were driven 108 feet into the ground; 187 such pillars were based on solid rock called the Niagara Shelf, which runs all the way to Niagara Falls. Then, and only then, the Prudential Building rose, and it is still standing today. The Sears Tower, the tallest building in the world, now joins the other skyscrapers.

Solid rock must be the foundation of our faith. That's what Isaiah 44:8 means: "Is there any god besides me? There is no other rock." Jesus watched the multitudes depart from him because the message he brought was not always a fair-weather message. Finally, he said to the twelve who stayed with him, "Do you also wish to go away?" They answered, "To whom can we go? You have the words of eternal life" (John 6:67-68).

Paul writes about people who go to those who will tell them exactly what they want to hear (II Tim. 4:3). There is a cartoon that illustrates it another way. The usher says to the preacher, "Ever since you've been telling it like it is, the offerings aren't what they were." There always will be proclaimers of a simplistic, fair-weather faith that is not equal to the storms of life. During such times, it is easy to reject such a flawed faith as being the real thing. How sad! When the elevator is out of order, we say we don't care—we didn't need it anyway. We can say that, but it doesn't help.

Finding an Alternate Route

If I needed to get someplace badly enough and the elevator was out of order, I might seek an alternate route. I might take the stairs. Sometimes we need to do that with our faith. Sometimes our routine actions become stale and, when tested, seem to fail us.

When I was growing up, my prayer life and much of what I believed were governed by what I was taught. Later in my life, my prayers and beliefs were inadequate in moments of crises. This led me to a serious study of the Bible—studying it with an open mind and a passion for learning. That new and alternate route led me into some questions that never have been resolved. Yet their very ambiguity allowed me to find a new avenue to God.

Some people have given themselves to good causes as a way of expressing faith. These disciples of the book of James cry, "Show me your faith apart from your works, and I by my works will show you my faith" (James 2:18). When they grow weary of well-doing and the forces of evil seem as strong as ever, they need to find an alternate route through some traditional spiritual discipline. The opposite is also true. Those with powerful spiritual disciplines who find the channels of communication being clogged up need to get out among God's children and serve. Look for the new avenues, the new elevators. Don't always try to rush back to something from your childhood.

A pastor I knew once preached a sermon in which he used dinosaurs to illustrate the importance of change. He said, "The dinosaur—whatever happened to the dinosaur? Who destroyed him? Do you want to know what destroyed the dinosaur? Nothing. The climate around him changed, and the dinosaur didn't change, and he died." Sometimes when our beliefs break down, we need to move in new directions to find that which is so important.

Learning to Wait

Finally, there are times when we simply have to wait. This is probably the hardest thing to do. We stand by an elevator that is broken down, knowing somebody will need to come and repair it. If the destination is high enough, we don't really have much choice except to wait.

We're not good at waiting, are we? Everything must be instant—instant breakfast, instant pain relief, instant cash. But that doesn't always work with faith. God is not a bellboy who will jump to our beck and call. We grow toward God. Isaiah said it well: "Those who wait for the LORD shall renew their strength, they shall mount up with wings like eagles, they shall run and not be weary, they shall walk and not faint" (40:31). Wait, I say. Wait for the Lord.

In the last days of his imprisonment, Dietrich Bonhoeffer, who was hanged by Hitler at Flossenburg just before the end of World War II, wrote these words to his friend Bethge, whom he never saw again:

> Please don't ever get anxious or worried about me, but don't forget to pray for me—I'm sure you don't. I am sure of God's guiding hand that I hope I shall always be kept in that certainty. You must never doubt that I'm travelling with gratitude and cheerfulness along the road where I'm being led. My past life is brim-full of God's goodness, and my sins are covered by the forgiving love of Christ cruci-

fied. Forgive my writing this. Don't let it grieve or upset you for a moment, but let it make you happy.

Bonhoeffer knew what it means to wait upon the Lord.

The Good News

What do you do when the elevator is out of order? What do you do when the beliefs you've held do not seem to sustain you in your moment of crisis, in the deep despair that comes when nothing seems to be going right in your life? Well, you can curse, or you can say it doesn't matter (but these reponses will not make things right); or you can struggle to find a different avenue, or you can wait.

The promise is there throughout the Bible: Even when we are frustrated by our inability to reach God, God comes down to touch and repair our lives. God is with us. "There is no other rock; I know not one" (Isa. 44:8). When we are not able to do anything through our own efforts, God understands our desire and our desperation, and God meets our need.

Chapter Nine

Stuck Between Floors

It has never happened to me. I have never been on an elevator that ground to a halt between floors. After talking to people who have been in a stuck elevator, I understand why they put telephones in elevators. When you're stuck, all you want to do is call for help! And there seems to be little else to do but wait for that help. You can't go up or down, and you can't escape.

That describes the way a lot of people feel about their lives. There may not be much wrong in their lives. They may not feel a sense of danger. It's just that, at the present moment, life doesn't seem to have any direction, any sense of purpose. They are stuck between floors.

It can happen when the routine of our lives becomes so pervasive that we feel as if we are suffocating. We get up at the same time, do the same things, see the same people, engage in the same small talk. To paraphrase part of Melvin Williams' folk song about suburbia:

> And we all get put in boxes,
> And we all look just the same.

Sometimes we seem to be stuck between floors because we are at one of those junctions in our lives when change has to happen. We finish school, but we cannot find a job. We retire, but we've made no concrete plans for the future. Our kids leave home. A neighbor moves. A meaningful past cannot be recaptured, and the future still has no focus. We are stuck.

One person described this condition as trying to cross a river and discovering when you reach midstream that there is no longer a landing on the opposite shore; and when you look back, you see the dock break loose and head downstream.

It isn't that we are not living when we are "stuck between floors." We are, but we can't figure out *why*. We hear that proverbial pilot come over the intercom of our airliner and say, "There's good news and bad news. The bad news is, we are lost. The good news is, we are making very good time."

Making the Most of the Wait

A friend of mine was once in an elevator that was stuck between floors. He told me about his frustrating experience. He made a phone call on the emergency phone, and then he waited. He was assured that all would be OK and that he should be patient. So he tried. But waiting is never easy. In those "empty" moments, he thought of a verse from Isaiah: "Those who wait for the LORD shall renew their strength, they shall mount up with wings like eagles, they shall run and not be weary, they shall walk and not faint" (Isa. 40:31).

When we are stuck between the floors of life, one thing we can do to make the most of the wait is to draw close to God and God's Word. When we trust that God will renew our strength, we can make it through even the longest wait.

When Elijah was forced to flee from Jezebel, he went to Mount Horeb and waited for forty days and forty nights. Then the voice of God spoke in the "sound of sheer silence" (I Kings 19:12). After that, he was ready to return. In the first chapter of Galatians, Paul tells of going away, following his conversion experience, to wait before beginning his public ministry (1:13-25). Both these men were "between floors"; one chapter in life was closing, another was yet to begin. And both men came out of the waiting period renewed.

We can spend our time another way while we are stuck between the floors of life by looking for the meaning in every moment. Have you ever tried to figure out what percentage of any given week's time is made up of meaningful experiences? If you were to write your autobiography, how much of what happened to you this past week would be included? If life is to be consistently meaningful, it must be meaningful during our routine days—while we are waiting.

So often we waste precious opportunities by failing to make the most of the moment. I confess to being amazed by busy parents who tell me they don't have much time to give to their children, but what time they do give is "quality time." I resist the temptation to laugh. The best quality moments I have had with my children came in the midst of quantity time—and at the most unusual places. We have shared marvelous moments—for example, on long car trips. Other meaningful moments have come when, horror of horrors, we were watching a television show that sparked a conversation. Simple games that require little conversation lend themselves to incredibly memorable moments. It's a little like taking home movies. Occasionally you secure something worth sending in to those TV shows that specialize in home videos. For every clip so valued, there usually is a mile of film on the cutting room floor.

We can also find meaning in those "in between" times by becoming better listeners. We miss so much joy in life because we fail to really hear what others say. I remember a man I met early in my ministry who was a tool and die maker. He was wise beyond his education.

One day he told me that the trouble with the world is that there are not enough listeners.

He said, "You know, Joe, I've discovered that everyone has a story to tell, if they can only find someone who is willing to listen." I'm glad I heard that early in life. For one thing, it has made me more sensitive and less restive when hearing a long story that is far more interesting to the teller than to the listener! But more important, it has reminded me to open myself to new ideas, relationships, and experiences. Eldon Weisheit captures the meaning of this in "Coffee at Howard Johnson's":

> I do not want to seem ungrateful, Mr. Johnson (I cannot bring myself to call you Howard), but I do not care about your 28 flavors of ice cream. . . . I am not interested in your Wednesday fish fry—all you can eat for $1.19. . . . It is not your prompt service or your clever menu that brings me to your door. . . . But I'd come, Mr. Johnson, because I do not come alone. . . . Your tables become altars where the cup is shared. . . . Love absorbs spilled sins like your thirsty napkins. . . . On your neutral ground God becomes incarnate without the flutter of angelic wings.

When we are stuck between floors, we must make the most of the wait.

Taking Charge of the Future

One of the positive things about life is that we can take charge of the future. We not only know that our between-floors situation is temporary, but we also have the option of choosing a new floor when we get started again.

I met a woman in the backwoods of Sierra Leone. She was from Oregon, where she had taught at a university. She was now a Peace Corps worker, living in a two-room dirt-floor cottage with no electricity or running water and teaching nutrition to the women of the village.

I asked her how she happened to choose this life, and she responded, "I am divorced. My children have all left home, and I decided that I had to choose between having a mid-life crisis and a mid-life adventure. I chose the adventure."

My wife is a hospice volunteer. They don't have a waiting list. She was in one of those between-floors times when a circular addressed to "occupant" came seeking volunteers to be trained to help the terminally ill. She responded, and it has been one of the most demanding and rewarding experiences of her life.

I sometimes think of those four fishermen who were dropping their nets when Jesus came by. Do you suppose that their lives had gone stale, and they needed a nudge in a new direction to get moving? Jesus invited and they responded.

All of us have gifts that we either use or lose. When we are in the doldrums of an in-between time, it is a good time to take inventory. If you put the gifts you have on a vertical line and the needs of the world on a horizontal one, somewhere they will cross. That is where you should go when you start moving again.

Sometimes, at the point where our gifts and the world's needs meet, there will be formed a literal "cross." That was Jesus' experience. But Jesus assures us that he will sustain us, and that our reward will be great.

The Good News

We want life to be meaningful. We dislike being stuck between the floors of life. It's understandable. The good news is that there are opportunities to make life meaningful even between floors. We can use that time to plan the next steps of our lives. The best news of all is that we don't have to remain "stuck."

When you find yourself stuck between the floors of life, remember the words of Ralph Waldo Emerson:

To laugh often and much, to win the respect of intelligent people and the affection of children; to appreciate beauty, to find the best in others, to leave the world a bit better, whether by a healthy child, a garden patch or a redeemed social condition; to know even one life has breathed easier because you lived. This is to have succeeded.

We can miss meaningful moments of life everywhere, but we can also *find* them anywhere, even between floors.

Chapter Ten

When You Hit Bottom

'll never forget the elevator in a hotel where I once stayed. It serviced all floors above ground, but it also would stop in the basement, the sub-basement, and another level simply called "lowest level." Our car was parked in the garage on the last and lowest level. If I had maintained my childhood belief that heaven is up and hell is down, I would have been looking for asbestos underwear before pushing the button to retrieve my car! As it was, I never felt as far down as when I departed the elevator in that dimly lit, dank-smelling place. I was absolutely certain that I had dropped as far as I could without being below the water table!

What do you do when your elevator of life hits bottom; when all seems darkness around you; when no matter what you try, nothing seems to work? Try as you will, there is nothing in life that is what you intended it to be. You feel like that proverbial rock on the bottom of the ocean.

Bottoming Out

Most of us have had "hit bottom" experiences. Those who haven't, someday will. It doesn't seem to make much difference how we get there. Sometimes we know it's of our own doing. Paul sat blind in Damascus, as a result of his passion to destroy Christians. The prodigal son found himself in a pigpen in the far country, because of his bad choices. At other times, we are like innocent Job, sitting on a dungheap and wondering how such a thing could happen to him.

Fate is no respecter of persons. In *First, You Cry*, NBC spokesperson Betty Rollin tells about her experience with breast cancer. Early in her book, she writes optimistically: "Everything always worked out. I expected it to. In my life, deprivation, injustice, disease were as remote as Bangladesh . . . as unlikely as cancer." Then a lump in her breast turned out to be malignant. The surgeon performed a radical mastectomy, and she hit bottom.

Margaret Higgins won a Pulitzer prize for writing about men who fought in the Korean War. She was interviewing a Marine who was eating cold beans with a trench knife. His clothes were stiff as a board. She asked him, "If I were God, and I were to grant you one wish, what would you ask for?" He said, "I'd like to see tomorrow. That's what I'd ask for." That Marine knew what it felt like to "hit bottom."

It is not only tragic situations such as these, however, that drag us to the bottom emotionally. Often it is the simple grinding away of our dreams. We set out with such lofty hopes and expectations, but life has a way of frustrating them. We can sympathize with Willie Loman in *Death of a Salesman* when he lamented his lost dream of providing for his family: "Just once I wish I could have something paid for before it broke or wore out."

In her book *Hot Flashes*, Barbara Raskin wrote: "I've eliminated all expectations from my life. I haven't stopped living. I've only stopped expecting. I no longer want to be exposed to disappointment. I no longer want to be at risk. By eliminating expectations, I reduce the possible occasions for unhappiness to almost zero."

Even the heroes of scripture experienced this "bottoming out." Jeremiah pleaded with his people to repent, only to have them turn against him, beat him, and imprison him in a cistern (37:15-16). That's really hitting bottom! And Hosea discovered that his wife was unfaithful and had returned to her life of prostitution (2:2-6). Jesus knew the feeling as he hung on the cross. He lamented, "My God, my God, why have you forsaken me?" (Matt. 27:46).

Reaching Out

God often seems more real to us when we are at the bottom of the elevator shaft than when we are in the regular commerce of going up and down.

Many of the psalms, those great sensitive poems of ancient Israel, begin when the psalmist is at the bottom of the elevator of life. "My God, my God, why have you forsaken me?" is the way Psalm Twenty-two begins. Likewise, this is the first line of Psalm Thirteen: "How long, O LORD? Will you forget me forever?"

Then, as the psalmists struggled, words of hope began to leap out. Psalm Twenty-two concludes: "Future generations will be told about the Lord, and proclaim his deliverance to a people yet unborn, saying that he has done it." Another psalm ends this way: "I have trusted thy steadfast love."

Paul, in his blindness, felt the hand of Ananias touch him (Acts 9:17). The prodigal, in the pigpen, said, "I will get up and go to my father" (Luke 15:18). Job, sitting on a dungheap, cried out, "Now my eye sees you; therefore I despise myself, and repent in dust and ashes" (42:5b-6).

It is so easy to interpret a successful life as the fruits of our own labor. But when we hit bottom, when we fail, we know we need help. We need to reach out.

Moving Out of Despair

It is one thing to know that we need help and to be sensitive when it is offered; it is quite another to take the next step, and to move out of our despair. In Tennessee Williams' *Glass Menagerie,* it is pointed out to the physically and emotionally disabled sister that it doesn't take much to get yourself nailed up in a coffin, but in order to get out, one must begin by removing one nail.

It was once a custom in Russian villages, at a time when many children did not survive infancy, to have a mourning hut at the outskirts of every town. All women who lost children were sent to live in that hut for a month of solitude and grief. At the end of the month, the hut was set on fire. The woman inside had to decide whether to live or die. If she came out of the burning hut, this indicated that she was prepared to live, and she then rebuilt the hut for the next mourner. As harsh as the practice may sound to us, it provides a graphic picture of the necessity to decide to move out of the despair we find "at the bottom."

It is probable that nothing has happened to any of us that someone else has not already experienced. When we decide that we want to rise up from "the bottom," there are resources that can help us.

First, we can seek others who have had the same experiences we have had. Albert Schweitzer calls this "the fellowship of those who have known the mark of pain." There are long lists of organizations that have been formed because someone understood his or her own need. There are support groups for widows who have experienced the sudden death of a spouse, for parents who have lost a child, for recovering alcoholics and drug users, for those who are out of work—the list goes on and on. Sometimes all we need is the fellowship of the church of Jesus Christ, which undergirds us and moves us to find those people within it who bear the same "mark of pain" and can give us insight into it.

Second, we can turn to printed resources. The difficult situations we face and the methods of handling them are endless—as are the resources that have been written to help us cope with them. Once we recognize that we need help and make the decision to move out of our despair, we should turn to available resources that can assist us in this process. A pastor, a librarian, or a friend who has experienced the same problem can suggest appropriate resources.

Certainly the Bible carries within it the resources to move us out of the bottom of life. It gives its best help to those who have already lived with it. When we are familiar with the scriptures, they weave a net of the undergirding spirit of God that leaps to mind. Are we afraid of the future? So was Abraham. Do we feel like quarreling with God? So did Job. Do we feel the loss of a friend so badly that we need to cry? So did Jesus. Being familiar with these and other stories of the Bible gives our faith a strong foundation. Waiting until tragedy strikes to build this foundation is like building a house on sand: "Everyone who hears these words of mine and does not act on them will be like a foolish man who built his house on sand. The rain fell, and the floods came, and the winds blew and beat against that house, and it fell—and great was its fall!" (Matt. 7:26-27).

But we do not need to be scholars to access the help waiting for us in the Bible. There are many tools to help us understand and study the scriptures. And with time and practice, our skills increase. Just as one who is experienced in a particular craft no longer needs the instructions and is able to complete a project quickly, so one who is familiar with God's Word readily finds comfort and help.

Third, we can begin to soothe our souls and replace

our despair with hope with the help of music. Music is indeed a universal language that moves beneath our intellect and picks up our spirits. Someone once said that if words could communicate all our feelings, there would be no need for music. The beauty in music is its variety. Find your own. It may be classical or country, instrumental or vocal, but do find *your* music.

Using Our Pain

A story is told about the day Gene Stallings, football coach at the University of Alabama, was anxiously awaiting the arrival of his first son. When the news of the birth came from the doctor, Stallings was ecstatic, envisioning football, hunting, fishing, and other outdoor experiences they could share. Then the doctor handed him a bomb: "Your son has Down's Syndrome." At that moment Stallings went to the bottom of the elevator shaft. "He'll probably only live four years," the doctor told him. The news was difficult for Stallings, but he was determined that his son would have the happiest four years possible.

But four years did not end the boy's life. He continued to grow. In fact, he's still living, now age thirty. Today father and son sit together on the sidelines with the University of Alabama football team. Every time Stallings sees his son, his face lights up with pride and joy. He calls him a gift of God.

As the saying goes, when you are handed a lemon, make lemonade. That's what Betty Ford did when her family confronted her with the knowledge that she suffered from alcoholism. She went for the cure, and then she established a clinic for alcoholics.

When you hit bottom, how can *you* make your experience helpful to others?

The Good News

It is never too late. That is the good news. When you hit bottom, you need not stay there. Remember that promise!

In the Louvre in Paris, there is a painting called *Faust*. It is a painting of a chess game. On one side of the chess board is Mephistopheles, a manifestation of the devil. Opposite him is Faust, with whom he has made an infamous pact. Mephistopheles is pointing at the board with a heinous look of triumph. You can almost hear him say, "Checkmate!" Faust is cowering on the other side.

A Grand Master chess player was looking at this painting one day, feeling the despair of it, when suddenly he jumped at the painting and shouted, "Wait a minute! Wait a minute! Faust still has one move!"

That's the message. No matter how far down our elevator of life may take us, there's always one more move, through the gospel of Christ, that will lift us up and send us forth in strength!

Chapter Eleven

In Case of Fire, Use Stairs

I spend more time than I like to admit walking up and down stairs in buildings that have elevators. It really isn't my idea. I have a friend who has claustrophobia. The thought of being inside a tiny box with no windows sends her looking for the nearest stairway. Since I am married to this friend, I feel obliged to join her most of the time!

We have learned to compromise somewhere around five floors. Under five floors, we take the stairs. Over five floors, we use the elevator. Nothing I have said about the safety of well-lighted public elevators, in contrast to the dimly lit, isolated stairwells of most public buildings, has impressed her. As I puff up the tenth flight to the fifth floor, I point out to her that the danger of being hurt in a falling or stuck elevator pales in comparison to the ease of being mugged on those seldom-used stairways. She always holds a trump card on safety, though. She points to the sign that is required by law to be posted near every elevator: "IN CASE OF FIRE, USE STAIRS."

I remain unpersuaded. There may be movies about dangerous fires in tall buildings, but *I've* never been near one of those buildings when a fire broke out! Besides, I like the elevator. It has become a part of my life of ease, a part that I take for granted.

Taking Things for Granted

We live a cocoon-like existence, complacent with things as they are, and we find any change an intrusion into our way of living. A number of years ago, our government decided that we should join the rest of the world in measuring distance in kilometers rather than miles, and in selling gasoline by the liter rather than the gallon. You know what happened. We absolutely refused to go along with it! It had nothing to do with right and wrong. It had to do with change—change from our comfortable routine—and we would not have any part of it.

In 1873, a man named Sholes invented a machine we call the typewriter. What a wonderful invention! He arranged letters on keys to create a keyboard. We've been using the same keyboard ever since. We've grown accustomed to it. Perhaps we have said to ourselves that the keys were ordered just so to enable us to hit them more quickly—the most common letters to be struck by the strongest fingers. But that isn't true!

When Sholes invented the typewriter, the mechanics of it were so cumbersome that he had to find a way to slow down the fingers to prevent the keys from sticking. That's why he put the letters where he did—*to slow us down!* New keyboards have been designed and produced that are far more efficient, but we won't buy them because we won't change. We like things the way they are, and we take it for granted that things will remain that way.

We take a lot of things for granted. These things are part of the good things of life that are as normal as the air we breathe. Like the elevator, we expect to never have to worry about their availability.

Although we Americans have become more health conscious in recent years, we are still accustomed to eating what we want when we want. We want our fast food, red meat, sugar, junk food, and so forth. Don't bother me with too many lectures, we say. We want to enjoy life.

Health is a fragile thing, yet we take it for granted. We eat what we like until the doctor tells us that our arteries are clogged because we have consumed too much cholesterol, or until we notice that our vision is a little blurred and later discover that we are diabetic. We take our health for granted—as part of the good life—until we no longer have it.

And we take our families for granted until something happens to them. Our families are part of the good life, like the elevator. But families are fragile. A television commercial that always brought a lump to my throat was the one in which a young man said, "Sure, I planned to go to college. The thing I didn't plan on was my dad dying." Death, divorce, strained relationships—these are things we think will never happen to *our* family.

We also take our faith for granted. We talk about that old-fashioned religion that was good enough for mother, for father, for sister, or for brother, and we say it's good enough for us, too—until tragedy strikes.

In his book *Mass for the Dead*, William Gibson tells about his mother's death. He wanted to recapture for himself the sense of her faith. He went into her empty apartment and picked up her glasses and her dog-eared prayer book. He sat down in her chair and then said, "I couldn't hear what she'd heard. I couldn't see what she'd seen. I tried to stoke the fires of my dead mother's faith, and it never ever works that way."

It is in times of crisis or tragedy—"in case of fire"—

that all the things we take for granted seem to be useless. At those times, it's time to look for a stairwell!

Taking the Stairs

God is alive and available, just like those dependable stairs. We often cruise through life taking for granted the comforts of life that are exemplified by the elevator. But in case things don't work out as we've planned—"in case of fire"—we need to remember that our never-changing God is always available to us. God is a constant in this changing world.

There is a story of a harried music teacher who was greeted one morning by a friend with the words, "What's the good word today?" The teacher sighed, went over to her tuning fork, struck it once to create a tone, and said, "That note is A. That's the good word. It was A yesterday, is A today, and will be A tomorrow. The first-year piano students may murder their lesson. The bass may not be able to hit his low notes and the soprano her high notes. The alto may warble off-key. But that is still A."

God is that stable factor. God is the A note of our lives, the stairway of our changing existence.

One of the great twentieth-century preachers, G. A. Studdert-Kennedy, often spoke of his conversion. He stood one night on a moor beside the English Channel. His life had fallen apart. Yet he sensed a presence near him. A phrase from his military past came to him: "Who goes there?" He did not know what kind of answer he might receive, or even if there would be an answer. He said, "I made my cry, 'Who goes there?' And I got my answer. I have sometimes doubted it, have never wholly understood it, but it remains. I have been trying to say it ever since, one word—God."

We not only know that the stairs are there, but we also know that they are dependable. We know this because God revealed his true personality in Jesus of Nazareth. This means that we know the true nature of this God.

Is God concerned about individual people? Yes! Test this by considering Jesus' concern for people. His compassion for individuals knew no bounds. It ranged from the little children who came to be near him to widows, whose plight was always difficult in their society. He was moved to compassion by the plea of a hated Roman soldier of occupation, and he dealt kindly with a Samaritan woman of questionable character. Jesus was sensitive enough to the cries for help that he could feel someone touch the hem of his robe as he moved through a crowded street. He forgave sin and invited sinners to become followers.

When we say that God is like Jesus, we make a monumental statement. It means that God is as concerned about us as Jesus was about the people whose lives he touched. It means that God loves us and is concerned about us in spite of our looks, our social condition, and even our sinfulness.

Charles Bradlaugh, a famous atheist, once challenged H. P. Hughes, the head of the Rescue Mission of London, to a debate. Hughes agreed on one condition: that he could bring with him one hundred people who would tell what Jesus Christ had meant to them in life-crisis situations. Each would be willing to submit to cross-examination by any who doubted their stories. The minister invited his opponent to bring the same number, who would tell how their lack of faith had helped them in their time of need. On the day of the debate, Bradlaugh didn't show.

Countless stories can be told of those who discovered that in their moment of desperate need, God showed them the way to the stairs. The stairs are there, and the stairs are dependable. Our lives can be changed! Don't ever doubt it.

The Good News

The good news is that the stairs which beckon us when there is a fire are designed to get us out of the building. At the bottom of the stairwell, there is a doorway that leads to safety.

Isn't that what we want and need? It is nice to know that when we find our way to this faith of the God who was revealed in Jesus Christ, there is no way we can be caught up again in the shallow living we once took for granted. We have been set free. That's the promise of the gospel!

The true follower of Jesus willingly goes back into the building to share the good news—to tell others about the stairs. If indeed there is a fire, the true follower of Jesus helps others to safety and then helps to put out the fire. It is never enough for the Christian to simply escape from life. We are challenged to be a part of the change agent, to bring security to the whole building. That is where we will get our biggest thrill.

Once, when the pilot of a jumbo jet filled with passengers lowered the wheels to land at a busy airport, he discovered that one of the wheels did not come down. The plane circled while emergency preparations were made on the landing strip. Fire and ambulance equipment was standing by. As it turned out, the pilot was able to make a fairly comfortable landing, so the passengers did not need to make an emergency exit—much to their relief. As the passengers began to exit the aircraft, a Catholic priest said to one of the flight attendants, "Remember now, always, that the rest of your life is extra."

Those of us who have found the stairway in the emergencies of life know that, in some fashion, *all* of life is extra, a gift from God, because God is always with us—whether in the convenient and comfortable elevator or in the challenging stairwell!

Chapter Twelve

Express to the Top

I n the movie *Oh God*, God informs a grocery-store manager that he has been chosen to be the spokesperson to this age. He is invited to visit God's office on the thirteenth floor of a well-known building. When he tells God that there are only twelve floors in that building, God invites him to get on the elevator and see! Sure enough, the button panel includes a thirteenth button. He presses it, and the elevator opens up to a beautiful office where God, played by George Burns, is waiting.

After the meeting, the man returns to the ground floor by the same elevator and sees that the panel now has only twelve buttons. He is frightened, confused, and awed by the unexplainable thirteenth floor.

We know the feeling. We are told by the words of Jesus that there is another floor, and we are promised that we will meet God there. But we have neither seen nor experienced that floor; we know only the existing floors of our present life. When informed that such a floor is our final home, we are quick to respond that we are happy where we are and not in the least bit "homesick"!

There's no mystery in this life greater than the mystery of that unseen floor—of the completion of life as we know it here on earth, the experience called death. We don't even want to think about it. We are sympathetic to the court jester who displeased the mighty caliph of

Baghdad and was to be put to death. When the jester reminded the caliph of the many times he had been amus-
ing to him, the caliph relented a bit and told the jester he
would allow him to choose the way he would die. The
jester responded, "If it is all the same to you, I choose to
die by old age."

Death is a subject we don't like to hear about, talk
about, or even read about. That's why this chapter comes
at the end of this book. If you have joined me through
the ups and downs of life discussed in previous chap-
ters, then perhaps you will let me share with you some
comments about this part of life.

I can still remember sitting in class in seminary. I was
fresh out of college, having no experience in pastoring a
church, and I was listening to a seasoned teacher talk
about the rural church. He went to the chalkboard and
drew two country lanes intersecting. He put a little
country church at the crossroads, and behind that church
he drew a series of crosses. Then he said, "Friends, that
is the cemetery. Be sure before you leave here that you
have something to say about that cemetery, because if
you don't, you have nothing at all to say!"

The haunting words of Isaiah speak to anyone who
seeks to help people who have lost loved ones: "Comfort, O comfort my people, says your God. Speak ten-
derly to Jerusalem, and cry to her that she has served her
term, that her penalty is paid, that she has received from
the LORD's hand double for all her sins" (40:1-2). What
can we say about the cemetery and the unseen floor?

Death Is a Part of Life

In Robert Inman's novel *Old Dogs and Children,* one of
the characters tearfully asks the doctor whether her father is dying. "We're all dying," he answered, his voice
heavy with the twilight weariness of the many years he

had carried the worn black bag in and out of dim rooms. "We're all dying," he repeated. "It's the only way out."

Have you ever noticed how we avoid the "D" word? We try to soften its harsh sound by using euphemisms. We say, "He passed away." "She went to her reward." "She headed west."

A friend told me of going to a town where there seemed to be an unusually large number of elderly women with no husbands. When he inquired about it, he was told that the husbands had gone away. For a short time, my friend thought he had moved to a community where men were completely irresponsible. Then one day he discovered that the husbands hadn't gone far—only to the edge of the community, in that little plot of ground behind the church!

We die. You will die; I will die. If we live on this earth long enough, we will stand by the graves of many friends and family members who have preceded us in this event. We can't dismiss it or dodge it. We will pass through "the valley of the shadow of death"; we cannot bypass that part of the trip.

Death Is Not the Final Word

The reality of death may seem dismal, but death is not the last word. It is an event in life—a major event, no doubt—but it is just one of many significant occasions.

That was Jesus' promise to his followers on the night before he was crucified: "In my Father's house there are many dwelling places. If it were not so, would I have told you that I go to prepare a place for you?" (John 14:2). In other words, "In my Father's building there are many floors!" Some day you too will get on an express to the unseen floor. But be assured that the floor is there! If it were not so, Jesus would have told us so.

Death can be compared to graduation. While we are still in school, we know that someday we will graduate and leave this familiar place. We have some ideas about what it must be like to be out of school, but no concrete experience. We can only know that life goes on beyond graduation. When graduation comes, we leave. We have no other choice. We discover for ourselves a new world. And we would not want to return to what we were before we graduated. Like graduation, death is a transition of life, and we need not fear transitions.

Reinhold Niebuhr gave this beautiful analogy months after his father's death:

> As a child I once spent a day with my grandmother. Toward evening, a severe storm began. "Now how will you get home, child?" the old woman asked. But then my father came to fetch me. He had a big blue coat, as men wore at that time, and as we left he said, "Come under here." I slipped under the coat, grabbed his hand, and off we went. I couldn't see anything as we splashed through puddles and mire. I heard the rain and the thunderclaps and seized my father's hand and held it tightly. But I would have been a fool if I had complained that it was dark around me. After all, it was my father's coat, protecting me from the weather, that made it dark. Father saw the path; I knew that . . . and when the coat parted, we were at home! I looked into my mother's cheerful face and at our bright, warm room, and everything was as pleasant and cozy as only home can be! Of course, father had brought me home. Where else should he have brought me? So it is with our heavenly Father. If only we trust Him, He holds our hand, takes us under His wings and leads us through storm and tempest.

It is with that kind of confidence that Paul writes: "I am convinced that neither death, nor life, nor angels, nor rulers, nor things present, nor things to come, nor powers, nor height, nor depth, nor anything else in all creation, will be able to separate us from the love of God in Christ Jesus our Lord" (Rom. 8:38-39). John Donne captured this promise in these lines: "One short sleep past, we wake eternally, And Death shall be no more: Death, thou shalt die!"

From Grief to Gratitude

Although we experience our own death only once, most of us will experience that of many others. When we celebrate All Saints Day in our churches, and the people are invited to stand in honor of ones they have loved and lost to death, few people remain in the pews.

If the one who died was very close to us, we cry. We feel hurt, lonely, disoriented. The tears are cleansing. They let us know how deeply we cared for that person. But the tears are basically for ourselves. We cry because our lives are changed, because we have lost a part of ourselves. We grieve, but in a very real sense, our grief is a gift we give to our departed loved one. Our loved one has been spared the experience of grieving our death.

The day after his wife of sixty years died, Harry Emerson Fosdick, then pastor emeritus of Riverside Church in New York City, confided in a friend: "I'm the one who had ailments, and I was afraid I'd die first and leave her alone. Now she's gone, and I will be the one to face loneliness. I'm so thankful for that. This is something I can do for Florence."

Thornton Wilder once said, "The highest tribute to the dead is not grief but gratitude." Knowing that death is a part of life and a part of God's plan, I am grateful for having been a part of the lives of those whose deaths I grieve. I find myself stopping to remember parents who loved me, teachers who challenged me, friends who enriched my life, and many acquaintances who shared the elevator with me for a floor or two!

The Good News

I visited the remarkable Kodak Museum in Rochester, New York, a few years ago. One display that demonstrated the power of the zoom lens captured my full attention. The first picture was of a scenic landscape in the Rocky Mountains. For the second picture, the camera was more narrowly focused. What had appeared in the first picture to be a spot at the foot of the mountain was actually a cabin. In the third picture, what had been a blurred outline in front of the cabin was now clearly a man seated in a chair on the front porch, reading a book. The final picture was a close-up of the man's wrinkled forehead, with a fly perched upon it. All this was photographed by one camera located in one place, but with different lenses.

I will never know whether that fly bothered the old man enough for him to finally take a swat at it. But I do know that in the first picture, the landscape, that fly is insignificant. When confronted in its immediacy, death is a terribly important event. But it must be kept in perspective.

I take great comfort when the writer of the Twenty-third Psalm speaks of "the valley of the shadow of death" (vs. 4). Up to that point, God is spoken of in third person: "He maketh me to lie down . . . he leadeth me . . ." But when writing of the valley, the psalmist says, "Thou art with me; thy rod and thy staff they comfort me" (KJV). This is the good news: that God is with us in the elevator of life—even as we are moving toward the unseen floor.

> One short sleep past, we wake eternally,
> And Death shall be no more: Death, thou shalt die!